A Pull Ahead Book

Indian Chiefs

Lynne Deur

Lerner Publications Company • Minneapolis, Minnesota

ACKNOWLEDGMENTS: The illustrations are reproduced through the courtesy of: pp. 3, 30, Chicago Historical Society; pp. 7, 12, 39, 46, 56, Independent Picture Service; pp. 8, 33, 41, 47, 78, Library of Congress; p. 14, Detroit Historical Museum; p. 17, New York Public Library, I. N. Phelps Stokes Collection; p. 20, New York State Historical Association, Cooperstown; pp. 23, 24, 32, 34, 38, 63, 72, 76, 81 (top), 88, 89, 90, 94, 96, 99, 103, Smithsonian Institution National Anthropological Archives, Bureau of American Ethnology Collection; pp. 29, 59, 95, *Dictionary of American Portraits*, Dover Publications, Inc.; p. 40, "The Trail of Tears" by Robert Lindneux, from the original oil painting in Woolaroc Museum, Bartlesville, Oklahoma; pp. 42, 53, 58, National Collection of Fine Arts, Smithsonian Institution; p. 48, University of Miami, Florida, Mark F. Boyd Collection; p. 50, Illinois State Historical Library; p. 60, W. H. Over Dakota Museum, The University of South Dakota; p. 64, U. S. Signal Corps, National Archives; p. 65, Northern Pacific Railway Company; p. 68, "Custer's Last Stand" by Edgar Paxson, Whitney Gallery of Western Art; p. 71, Travel Section, South Dakota Department of Highways; pp. 74-75, "The Battle of Little Bighorn" by Kicking Bear, Southwest Museum; p. 80, Nebraska State Historical Society; p. 81 (bottom), Museum of the American Indian, Heye Foundation; pp. 83, 92, 93, Western History Collection, University of Oklahoma Library; p. 84, Arizona Pioneers' Historical Society; p. 102, Buffalo Bill Historical Center.

Front Cover: *Chief Black Hawk* (right) *and His Son*, painted by John Jarvis in 1833, Thomas Gilcrease Institute of American History and Art, Tulsa, Oklahoma.

Back Cover: Geronimo (front) and other Apache prisoners of war at Fort Bowie, Arizona, 1886, U.S. Signal Corps, National Archives.

LIBRARY OF CONGRESS CATALOGING IN PUBLICATION DATA

Deur, Lynne.
   Indian Chiefs.

   (A Pull Ahead Book)
   SUMMARY: Biographies of thirteen American Indian leaders who tried to halt the gradual destruction of their people.

   1. Indians of North America—Biography—Juvenile literature. [1. Indians of North America—Biography] I. Title.

E89.D39 1972   970.1'9022[920]   75-128807
ISBN 0-8225-0461-8

International Standard Book Number: 0-8225-0461-8
Library of Congress Catalog Card Number: 75-128807

Fourth Printing 1979

contents

A 50-foot statue of Black Hawk in the town of Oregon, Illinois. *(Courtesy Chicago Historical Society)*

NEZ PERCÉ

SIOUX
Teton

OTTAWA

CHEYENNE

FOX SAUK

IROQUOIS
Mohawk

WAMPANOAG

SHAWNEE

CHEROKEE

APACHE

CREEK

SEMINOLE

The map above shows the tribes of the Indian chiefs in this book. The map below shows the wars and important battles they fought or inspired. The chiefs came from different tribes and lived in different times, but they all shared one goal—to halt the white man's advance over North America.

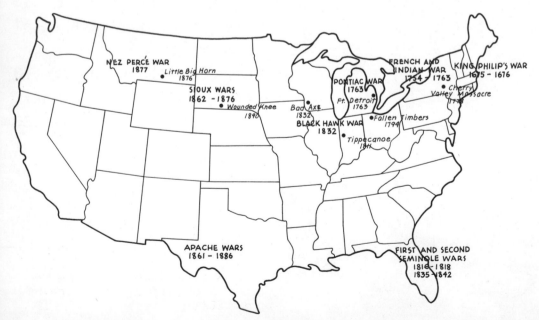

NEZ PERCÉ WAR
1877

Little Big Horn
1876

SIOUX WARS
1862 –1876

PONTIAC WAR
1763

FRENCH AND
INDIAN WAR
1754 – 1763

KING PHILIP'S WAR
1675 – 1676

Cherry
Valley Massacre
1778

Ft. Detroit
1763

Wounded Knee
1890

Bad Axe
1832

Fallen Timbers
1794

BLACK HAWK WAR
1832

Tippecanoe
1811

APACHE WARS
1861 – 1886

FIRST AND SECOND
SEMINOLE WARS
1816 –1818
1835 –1842

5

Indian Patriots and White Savages

All of the Indian leaders in this book were involved in some part of the American Indian's long struggle to defend himself against the foreign invasion of the white man. Like a large number of the world's heroes, many of these chiefs were military leaders and fighting men. But some were statesmen, inventors, religious leaders, or educators. Some were not really chiefs (heads of tribes), but did so much to help their people that they became as important as chiefs. All of these leaders tried in some way to stop the gradual, terrible destruction of their people.

Unfortunately, too many Americans, white and red, have been taught to see Indian heroes as villains. In general the Indian point of view has been ignored, and few people have understood that the red man had good reason to fight. Men like King Philip, Black Hawk, Osceola, Crazy Horse, and Cochise were Indian patriots. But stories, movies, and even history books have made them look like bloodthirsty savages.

Actually, the Indian was no more brutal than the white man. Whites have pointed again and again to the Indian practice of scalping as proof that Indians were savages. Yet white men took scalps too. In 1755 Governor William Shirley of Massachusetts Bay Colony even offered bounties for the scalps of Indian men, women, and children.

White men were guilty of other savagery as well. Many famous Indian-fighters were proud of their reputations as "squaw killers." The general who captured Osceola, leader of the Seminoles, seized him under a white flag of truce. The massacre of Indian men, women, and children at Wounded Knee was more brutal than the massacre of Colonel Custer and his troops at the Battle of the Little Bighorn. Then there were the paper brutalities—the treaties and promises made and broken again and again. And finally, after robbing the Indians of their land, their religion, their way of life, and their future as a people, the white man herded the red men onto reservations where he savagely took advantage of them whenever it was convenient.

Today the Indians, along with other oppressed minority groups, are struggling to gain equal rights in this land and regain their pride as a people. It is time for Indian heroes and leaders to take their rightful place in our nation's history.

By His EXCELLENCY

WILLIAM SHIRLEY, Esq;

Captain-General and Governor in Chief, in and over His Majesty's Province of the *Massachusetts-Bay*, in *New-England*, and Vice-Admiral of the same, and Major-General in His Majesty's Army.

A PROCLAMATION.

 HEREAS the Indians of *Norridgewock*, *Arresagun-a-ook*, *Weweenock* and *St. John's* Tribes, and the Indians of the other Tribes inhabiting in the Eastern and Northern Parts of His Majesty's Territories of *New-England*, the *Penobscot* Tribe only excepted, have, contrary to their solemn Submission unto His Majesty long since made and frequently renewed, been guilty of the most perfidious, barbarous and inhuman Murders of divers of his Majesty's *English* Subjects ; and have abstained from all Commerce and Correspondence with His Majesty's said Subjects for many Months past ; and the said *Indians* have fully discovered an inimical, traiterious and rebellious Intention and Disposition ;

I have therefore thought fit to issue this Proclamation, and to Declare the Indians of the Norridge-wock, Arresaguntacook, Weweenock and St. John's Tribes, and the Indians of the other Tribes now or late inhabiting in the Eastern and Northern Parts of His Majesty's Territories of New-England, and in Alliance and Confederacy with the above-recited Tribes, the Penobscots only excepted, to be Enemies, Rebels and Traitors to his Most Sacred Majesty : And I do hereby require His Majesty's Subjects of this Province to embrace all Opportunities of pursuing, captivating, killing and destroying all and any of the aforesaid Indians, the Penobscots excepted.

AND WHEREAS the General Court of this Province have voted, That a Bounty or Encouragement be granted and allowed to be paid out of the Publick-Treasury to the marching Army that shall be employed for the Defence of the Eastern and Western Frontiers from the Twenty-fifth of this Month of *June* until the Twenty-fifth of *November* next ;

I have thought fit to publish the same ; and I do hereby promise, That there shall be paid out of the Province-Treasury to all and any of the said Forces, over and above their Bounty upon Enlistment, their Wages and Subsistence, the Premiums or Bounties following, viz.

For every Male Indian Prisoner above the Age of Twelve Years, that shall be taken and brought to *Boston*, *Fifty Pounds.*

For every Male Indian Scalp, brought in as Evidence of their being killed, *Forty Pounds.*

For every Female Indian Prisoner, taken and brought in as aforesaid, and for every Male Indian Prisoner under the Age of Twelve Years, taken and brought in as aforesaid, *Twenty-five Pounds.*

For every Scalp of such Female Indian or Male Indian under Twelve Years of Age, brought as Evidence of their being killed, as aforesaid, *Twenty Pounds.*

GIVEN under my Hand at Boston, in the Province aforesaid, this Twelfth Day of June, 1755, *and in the Twenty-eighth Year of the Reign of our Sovereign Lord Lord* GEORGE *the Second, by the Grace of* GOD, *of Great-Britain,* France, *and* Ireland, KING, *Defender of the Faith, &c.*

By His Excellency's Command,
J. WILLARD, Sec'y.

W. Shirley.

GOD Save the KING.

"Courtesy Pioneer Historical Society"

BOSTON: Printed by *John Draper*, Printer to His ' the Honourable His Majesty's COUNCIL. 1755.

Europeans said they were horrified by scalping, but they paid money for the scalps of their enemies. This 1755 proclamation offered £40 in British money for the scalp of an adult Indian male, £20 for the scalp of an Indian woman or child.

King Philip

King Philip

From the summer of 1675 to the summer of 1676 terror ruled in the New England colonies. Time and time again, bands of angry Indians attacked the settlements. They destroyed crops and villages and killed men, women, and children. Leading the attackers was a tall, proud Indian called King Philip.

No one is sure when Philip was born. It is certain, however, that he was the son of Massasoit, a famous Wampanoag chief. Shortly after the landing of the Pilgrims, Massasoit signed a peace treaty with Governor John Carver. And for 40 years he faithfully kept this treaty of peace with the colonists. Legend also says that he attended the first Thanksgiving. Evidently the chief greatly admired white men. He even presented his young sons to the governor of Massachusetts Bay Colony, asking the governor to give them English names. From then on the older son was called Alexander. The younger boy, Metacomet, became known as Philip.

In 1662, after the deaths of Massasoit and Alexander, Philip became chief of the Wampanoags. But he did not share his father's ideas about the white man. To Philip it seemed that the colonists were moving inland too quickly. Game was no longer as plentiful as it once was. The colonists were taking up land that the Indians needed for their hunting grounds. Philip feared that one day his people would be destroyed. Other Indian leaders felt the same way, and soon the young chief became the head of an alliance of several tribes. These Indians had guns and knew how to use them.

But even though he did not like or trust white men, Philip continued to keep an uneasy peace with the colonists for 13 years. During that time the colonists did not trust Philip either. They knew that this proud, handsome chief had great leadership abilities. In time they called him "King" Philip because of his proud manner and his love of fine clothes.

Then, early in the winter of 1675, an Indian warrior who spied for the colonists was found dead in a pond near Plymouth. The colonists assumed he had been killed by his tribesmen. Quickly they sought revenge. In June 1675 they tried and executed three of Philip's warriors. But the Indians felt that they should have handled the problem. The colonists of Plymouth had interfered. Angry Indians gathered in Philip's village, and some of them wandered into the colonists' nearby town, Swansea. They shot a few cows, scared the settlers out of their homes, and looted the town. A young boy shot at one of the Indians. A day later the warriors struck back. King Philip's war had begun.

Throughout the summer and fall of 1675 the Indians attacked border settlements. They destroyed crops and cattle and killed hundreds of whites, including women and children. Philip was becoming more and more confident of his success. Surely he would drive these foreigners back across the sea!

The Indians' success was soon to end, however. A force of 1,000 men seized a major Indian fort in Rhode Island. An Indian scout guided them across a wild ice-covered marsh until they came to the island fort, which was hidden by piles of branches and underbrush. Breaking through the tangled shelter, the colonists fought until dark, set fire to the Indians' lodges, and killed hundreds of warriors, women, and children.

King Philip lies dead, having been shot in the back. After the chief's death in 1676, King Philip's War ended in total defeat for the Indians of southern New England.

Early in the spring of 1676 the Indians struck back. But soon it was time for planting and fishing, and some of them left the war camps and went home. The colonists organized their forces with even greater energy and took on additional volunteers and groups of Indians who had left Philip. They raided the warriors' hideouts, destroyed Indian cornfields, and captured women and children. They promised to pardon all warriors who would desert Philip.

It was clear that King Philip was defeated, and he himself knew it. Yet he continued to fight. In August of 1676 the chief was shot in the back by one of his own warriors who had decided to join the colonists. Philip's wife and child were captured and later sold into slavery.

The man the colonists saw as cruel and savage was dead. It is true that he had left a trail of terror. Thirteen villages and 600 buildings had been destroyed, and 700 colonists in Massachusetts, Connecticut, and Rhode Island were dead. But on the other hand, the colonists were not unhappy to have a reason to drive the Indians out of southern New England. They had wanted more land for settlement and war was a quick way to get it.

Although the colonists could see Philip's savagery clearly, they did not see their own. They even cut the chief's head from his dead body and placed it on a pole. Then the colonists paraded victoriously through Plymouth with it. Later they placed the head on display. There in Plymouth, the settlement befriended by Massasoit, the skull of King Philip stared blankly at its curious viewers for 25 years.

Pontiac
(Courtesy Detroit Historical Museum)

Pontiac

The French and Indian War (1754-1763) made great changes in the course of American history. England gained a vast amount of land by defeating the French and Indian troops. After the war, she owned all the territory from the eastern seacoast to the Mississippi River, except for New Orleans. She also claimed a large part of what is now Canada.

The Indians west of the Allegheny Mountains were alarmed by the changes that the war brought about. The French had always treated them fairly. Often they provided the Indians with food and ammunition. But the British were different. They did little to make friends with the Indians. And settlers from the English colonies were beginning to cross the Alleghenies to build homes and farms. The Indians' hunting grounds were in danger.

Pontiac, chief of the Ottawa Indians, was very angry when the English took over his territory in 1760. Born in about 1720 in what is now northwest Ohio, Pontiac had fought with the French against the English. When it became clear that the French were accepting defeat, Pontiac decided that the Indians should carry on the fight. He felt that a few Indian victories might bring the French back into the struggle. (The fighting was over, but the French and British had not yet signed a peace treaty.) And, if all the tribes united, it even seemed possible that the Indians by themselves could keep back the English.

In 1761 Pontiac started to organize many Indian tribes. His alliance included tribes from the Great Lakes southward to the Gulf of Mexico—Ottawas, Hurons, Delawares, Shawnees, Kickapoos, Chippewas, and Senecas. The Indians had two goals. First they wanted to destroy all British forts west of the Alleghenies. Then they would destroy the homes of settlers and the camps of traders in the same region.

Fort Detroit, 1794. This frontier settlement grew into the city of Detroit, Michigan.

Pontiac and his warriors planned to take Fort Detroit. In May 1763 they asked for a meeting with the British commander and entered the fort with weapons hidden under their blankets. But the commander had been warned of the plot, and Pontiac could tell that the fortress was heavily guarded and ready for trouble. Confused and angry, Pontiac and his followers left the fort. Several times during the next few days the Indians tried to enter Fort Detroit, but the clever young commander prevented each attempt. Finally, on May 9, Pontiac decided to besiege the fort. His forces surrounded Detroit and held it under siege for six months. But they were not able to drive the British out.

In other areas the Indians were more successful. By late June they had captured every British fort in the Ohio Valley-Great Lakes region, except Detroit and Fort Pitt. (Pitt was also under siege.) Along the frontiers of Pennsylvania, Maryland, and Virginia, they destroyed homes and crops. Men, women and children were killed or captured.

However, the Indians' success was brief. Several tribes dropped out of the Indian alliance after losing battles. Then news came that France and England had signed a peace treaty in February of 1763. There was no longer any hope of bringing the French back into battle. Colonial militias and fresh British troops entered the conflict, and in August the British broke the siege at Fort Pitt. Pontiac's men still encircled Fort Detroit. But during the autumn, band after band of them made peace and departed. Finally Pontiac himself with his remaining forces left Detroit, and the siege ended. Pontiac camped in Indiana for the winter and then spent many months traveling from tribe to tribe, trying again to build up support. He had no luck.

By 1765 it was clear to Pontiac that there was no chance of another uprising. That fall he agreed to come to a council at Detroit. There he declared his allegiance to the King of England. Throwing his wampum belt to the ground, he reportedly said, "By this belt I remove all evil thoughts from my heart. Let us live together as brothers." From the council he retired to a camp near his birthplace.

Pontiac was not seen again by white men until 1769. In that year he visited a trading post near St. Louis, Missouri. His visit was brief. An Indian warrior, legend says, sank a tomahawk into the chief's skull, then stabbed him in the back.

Some historians today think that Pontiac was not as important in the Indian alliance as he was long believed to have been. Yet his name continues to be linked with the greatest Indian confederation in American history.

Joseph Brant

Joseph Brant

In 1778, during the American Revolution, the little village of Cherry Valley, New York, was taken by storm. About 200 British troops and 600 Indians swarmed into the town. They slaughtered about 50 soldiers and male settlers, captured 70 women and children, and burned most of the village. The raid became known in history as the Cherry Valley Massacre.

Leading the Indian forces at Cherry Valley was a Mohawk chief named Joseph Brant. His battle tactics at the village and in other raids during the war earned him the nickname "Monster" Brant. Strangely enough, Brant was at the same time winning a reputation as a religious man.

Joseph Brant was born in 1742, probably somewhere in New York state. His tribe—the Mohawk—was one of the Five Iroquois Nations. His Indian name was Thayenda-negea. When the Mohawk leader was still a boy, his sister married a British general, Sir William Johnson. Brant's new brother-in-law sent him to a school for Indians in Connecti-cut, where Joseph learned to read and write English. Brant was also converted to Christianity and became a member of the Church of England.

Brant spent most of his life either fighting wars or carrying on missionary work among his people. At the age of 13 Brant fought with the British in the French and Indian War. Later he again fought with the British in the Pontiac War of 1763. Brant's greatest military achievements, however, came during the Revolutionary War. As a colonel in the British army, he commanded Iroquois forces that raided settlements in the Mohawk valley. One of these raids was the attack on Cherry Valley.

As a missionary, besides converting Indians to Christianity, Brant translated the Episcopal Book of Common Prayer and the Gospel of Mark into the Mohawk language. He also established the first Episcopal church in Canada, where he made his home after the Revolution.

Chief Brant was famous as a military leader
and as a Christian missionary.

Like other chiefs of his time, Joseph Brant dreamed of
establishing an Indian state west of the Alleghenies. Perhaps his ideas did not differ very much from Pontiac's,
except that Brant saw himself as chief of such a state. And
Brant felt certain the British would support him. But when
he traveled to England to make his request for support, the
British refused it. Furthermore, several leading Indian
chiefs were not willing to join themselves with Brant. His
plans for an Indian state never got off the ground. In 1807
the Mohawk chief died at his home in Canada.

Tecumseh

Tecumseh

Tecumseh was a handsome man and a powerful speaker. The Shawnee chief was also a man of character who stood firmly by his ideals. Many believe Tecumseh was the greatest Indian leader of them all.

Tecumseh was born in 1768 near what is now Springfield, Ohio. He grew up hating white men. Throughout his childhood the Shawnees were almost constantly fighting with white colonists along the Kentucky-Ohio border. During the 1770s settlers and armies crossed the mountains to take over land and to push the Indians from their hunting grounds south of the Ohio River. Tecumseh's father, war chief of a small Shawnee tribe, was murdered by whites when he refused to guide their hunting expedition. The fatherless boy faced further tragedy in 1780 when white men burned his village, forcing the Shawnees to scatter. White men also killed two of Tecumseh's brothers in battle. In addition, an old Shawnee chief who had treated him as a son was blamed for the death of two white men and was executed.

After the Revolution, Britain yielded the land north of the Ohio River to the United States. This land, which was called the Northwest Territory, was under American control. But the land did not actually belong to the United States until she made treaties with the Indians who lived there. White settlers ignored this fact and moved into the region. The Indians tried to fight them back. When Tecumseh was about 15 he helped attack boatloads of pioneers on the Ohio River. Later he led his own band of warriors against the whites.

Tecumseh proved himself a brave and daring fighter in the Battle of Fallen Timbers. (The battle was fought on a field littered with fallen tree trunks.) However, the battle lasted only about 40 minutes. Major General "Mad Anthony" Wayne and his 3,000 troops defeated the force of about 1,400 Indians. Several months after Fallen Timbers, in the spring of 1795, General Wayne called the defeated Indians together at the town of Greenville, Ohio. There he had them sign a treaty yielding large areas north of the Ohio

River to the United States. Tecumseh did not come to the meeting. Afterwards he declared the Treaty of Greenville unjust. The land, he claimed, was owned by all Indians. It could not be given or sold by a few chiefs. And since the land was owned by all Indians, why shouldn't all Indians unite as one nation? United, he believed, they could defeat the American troops in battle. The Indians could live in peace with both the United States and Canada—after they once proved their strength.

Within a few years Tecumseh's feelings about white people were changed somewhat by his friendship with Rebecca Galloway, a young white girl. Rebecca helped him improve his English and read aloud to him from the Bible, the works of Shakespeare, and European history books. She also taught Tecumseh something about the white man's ways of thinking. Tecumseh fell in love with Rebecca, but she refused to marry him unless he would live like a white man. Tecumseh thought it over but finally decided that he had to remain an Indian.

By this time Tecumseh's dream of a united Indian nation was uppermost in his mind. His brother, Tenskwatawa, helped bring his dream to the attention of other tribes. Once, in a trance, Tenskwatawa thought he saw the Indian Master of Life. The Master told him to give up drink and idleness. Tenskwatawa obeyed. Soon he was proclaiming his vision to anyone who would listen. He became known as the Shawnee Prophet. Then Tenskwatawa began to declare that Indians could gain their salvation only by returning to the ways of their ancestors. All the customs of white men had to be rejected. The Prophet's fame spread from tribe to tribe when he correctly predicted that on a certain day the moon would pass in front of the sun. The amazed Indians, who did not yet understand eclipses, were certain that the Prophet spoke nothing but truth.

Tenskwatawa, known as the Shawnee Prophet, shared his brother Tecumseh's dream of creating a united Indian nation.

In 1808 Tecumseh and his brother set up a village on the west bank of the Tippecanoe River in Indiana Territory. From there Tecumseh traveled in all directions, preaching to tribe after tribe. He told them that the best way to stop the advancing settlers was to form a united Indian nation. Tecumseh's powerful speeches (plus the Prophet's promise to make white men's bullets harmless) won the support of many tribes. Some of the old chiefs were doubtful. But young warriors were eager to join Tecumseh.

While Tecumseh was away, William Henry Harrison, governor of the Indiana Territory, called together a group of older chiefs. Harrison served the Indians several rounds of drinks. Then he had them sign away three million acres of land in Indiana. Tecumseh found out about the sale while he was still on the road. In August 1810 he met with Harrison in Vincennes, the territorial capital. There he made a strong speech of protest: "Sell a country! Why not sell the air, the clouds and the great sea, as well as the earth? Did not the Great Spirit make them all for the use of his children?"

Tecumseh threatens William Henry Harrison, governor of the Indiana territory. Tecumseh was furious when he heard the governor had tricked Indians into signing away 3 million acres of land. *(Courtesy Chicago Historical Society)*

In 1811 Tecumseh made a second long trip to gain support for his confederation. While he was gone, Governor Harrison and 1,000 men marched to the outskirts of Tecumseh's Indian village and camped there for the night. At dawn on November 7, 1811, the Shawnee Prophet and his warriors attacked the militia. They were driven back and scattered by Harrison's troops, who then set fire to the Indian village. From this small battle at the Tippecanoe River Harrison won lasting fame and, in 1840, the presidency of the United States. Tecumseh's dreams for a united Indian nation were destroyed.

Tecumseh in the uniform of a British officer. He served as a brigadier general for the British during the War of 1812.

Furious with his brother and broken in spirit, Tecumseh traveled to Canada to make his home. But the War of 1812 between England and the United States brought the Shawnee new hope. Surely the Indians and the British together could defeat the United States. Tecumseh joined the British and was given the rank of brigadier general. He recruited some 32 tribes to fight as British allies. Tecumseh's own army of about 3,000 men made up one of the greatest forces ever commanded by an Indian. Unlike most Indian leaders, he demanded that all of his prisoners be well treated.

But Tecumseh's cause was again lost. Despite their powerful Indian allies, the British were unable to defeat the Americans. During an eastward retreat with British troops

Tecumseh (at right, with tomahawk raised) was killed by a member of the victorious American army at the Battle of the Thames, 1813.

along Lake Erie, Tecumseh's army met the pursuing Americans in battle near the Thames River in Ontario. The British commander leaped into his carriage and headed east, leaving his troops to surrender. Tecumseh is said to have exchanged his British uniform for Indian buckskins. Then he continued to direct the battle. Badly wounded, he rushed with tomahawk in hand toward a fallen American soldier, and was fatally shot. The commander of the victorious American forces was again William Henry Harrison.

Tecumseh's warriors buried their chief secretly. The grave has never been found. Without a leader, his confederation fell apart. The Old Northwest was open to white settlement. From then on, each tribe or small group of tribes had to deal with the settlers on their own.

Sequoyah, holding a copy of the Cherokee alphabet he invented.

Sequoyah

Sequoyah was not an Indian chief, but he was a great leader of his people. He spent much of his life working to help the Cherokees and to keep them together as one nation.

Sequoyah was born in Tennessee in about 1770. His father was a white trader and his mother was a Cherokee. But Sequoyah was, in a sense, all Cherokee. He spoke the Cherokee language and for many years knew nothing but the Cherokee way of life.

Sequoyah was also a cripple. His name in Cherokee meant "The Lame One." Yet he learned to use his hands very skillfully. He was a fine silversmith who made earrings, bracelets, and buckles with great patience and close attention to detail. Most of his work was sold to white men.

Until the War of 1812 Sequoyah worked as a silversmith and took great interest in his home and garden. But during the war he served in the U.S. Army and lived and fought with white men. This seemed to change his life. For one thing, he saw his fellow soldiers reading and writing letters. Sequoyah came to feel it was important for his people to learn to read and write. Back home again, he became more aware of the troubles of his people. The Cherokees had made great efforts to adapt to the white man's civilization. Later they were to be known as one of the Five Civilized Tribes. But under pressure from the United States government, which was greedy for their land, families broke up and many Cherokees began to move westward. Sequoyah felt that a written language would help to hold his people together and make them stronger in dealing with the white man.

So Sequoyah set himself a difficult task. Educated white men had already tried—and failed—to set the Cherokee tongue into a written language. They said the task was impossible. But with some charcoal and some sycamore bark, Sequoyah began to work. For days, weeks, and months, he worked and thought. On his bark he tried to make a sign for each word in the Cherokee language. Sequoyah's family was not happy about his project. Their home and garden were suffering because Sequoyah spent all his time on his new work. One day, in a rage, Sequoyah's wife threw his sycamore bark into the fire. His work was destroyed. Furious, Sequoyah took his small daughter, then about six years old, and disappeared into the forest. The two of them traveled west to Arkansas, where some other Cherokees had already moved and settled.

Sequoyah began his work again one day when his daughter found a book someone had lost along the trail. From the book he learned the white man's secret. White men did not use a symbol for each word; instead, they used 26 signs, the letters of the alphabet, to make up words. Each sign stood for a sound in the language. Sequoyah knew that now he could succeed—by making a sign for each sound in the Cherokee language.

Cherokee Alphabet.

D a	R e	T i	δ o	O u	i v
S ga O ka	F ge	y gi	A go	J gu	E gv
σ ha	P he	θ hi	F ho	Γ hu	W hv
W la	C le	P li	G lo	M lu	$\mathfrak{A}$ lv
σ ma	OI me	H mi	$\mathfrak{I}$ mo	y mu	
Θ na t hna G nah	Λ ne	h ni	Z no	$\mathfrak{q}$ nu	O nv
T qua	ω que	P qui	V quo	ω quu	E quv
U sa oD s	4 se	b si	Φ so	$\mathcal{E}$ su	R sv
L da W ta	S de T te	J di J ti	V do	S du	$\mathfrak{F}$ dv
δ dla L tla	L tle	C tli	$\mathfrak{V}$ tlo	$\mathfrak{V}$ tlu	P tlv
G tsa	V tse	Ir tsi	K tso	J tsu	C tsv
G wa	ω we	Θ wi	$\mathcal{O}$ wo	ϑ wu	6 wv
ω ya	β ye	$\mathfrak{h}$ yi	h yo	G yu	B yv

Sequoyah's alphabet made it possible for the Cherokees to learn to read and write in their own language.

For several years Sequoyah worked on his new alphabet. During those years he also married a widow with a son. Sequoyah's new family was more understanding than his old one had been. In the evenings they sat together, testing his alphabet and working to improve it.

The masthead of *The Cherokee Phoenix*, a newspaper which Sequoyah helped to start in 1828.

Sequoyah's final test came about four years after he had left his first home. He and his daughter, Ah-yoka, returned east and met with a Cherokee council. The unbelieving council members gave Ah-yoka several sentences to write down. Then Sequoyah, who had been out of the room, returned and read aloud the sentences from Ah-yoka's paper. The Indian leaders were stunned, and then overjoyed. The Cherokees had a written language!

Sequoyah became the only person in the world to have invented a practical alphabet by himself. And thousands of the Cherokees learned to read and write within months after his alphabet was introduced. For his success the Cherokee Nation awarded him a medal and $500 a year for the rest of his life.

Sequoyah's work for his people did not end with the alphabet. In 1828 he helped establish a newspaper, *The Cherokee Phoenix*, written both in English and in Cherokee.

The Cherokees, as well as other southeastern tribes, were forced by the U.S. government to leave their homes and go to Oklahoma. The Indians suffered such hardships along the way that the path they followed became known as The Trail of Tears. *(Courtesy Wollaroc Museum)*

Ten years later, in 1838 when the United States government forced the Cherokee people to abandon their land in Georgia and move to Oklahoma, Sequoyah helped them to find new homes and tried to reunite them with Cherokees who had moved westward earlier. In 1842 he set off to search for a tribe of Cherokees said to have been lost many years before. A few years later his tribe received a message—written in Cherokee—telling them that Sequoyah had died in Mexico City in 1843.

This statue of Sequoyah, donated by the state of Oklahoma, stands in the Capitol in Washington, D.C.

Today a statue of Sequoyah stands in the Capitol in Washington, D.C. The giant redwood tree of California was named the sequoia in his honor. The written language formed from Sequoyah's alphabet did help to unify and strengthen the Cherokee Nation, even after their terrible march across the South to Indian Territory in Oklahoma. His gift was called "more valuable than a bag of gold in the pocket of every Cherokee."

Osceola

Osceola

The Cherokees were not the only Indians to be removed from the southeastern United States in the early 19th century. The Creeks, Choctaws, and Chickasaws—three other tribes in the group known to white men as the Five Civilized Tribes—were also removed to Indian Territory in Oklahoma. The Seminoles were the last of the Civilized Tribes to remain in the Southeast. And many Americans felt that the Seminoles too should be moved westward from their homes in Florida. Southern plantation owners especially wanted them gone. Slaves were escaping from plantations and finding better homes and masters among the Seminoles. But removing the Seminoles proved to be very difficult. It was accomplished only after two fierce wars. American troops had to deal with cunning leaders such as Osceola, described by one Indian agent as "a bold and dashing young chief . . . vehemently opposed to removal."

Osceola was born in Creek territory in Georgia in about 1804. Although his father was part white and he himself was fair-skinned, he denied being anything but Indian. As a child Osceola and his mother, along with a small group of Creek Indians, moved southward among the Seminoles. Soon the small, slim Osceola had proved himself a fine hunter and a good ballplayer. (The ball game of the Southeastern Indians—played with long-handled rackets—was an early form of lacrosse.)

At this time Florida still belonged to Spain. Near the end of the War of 1812 the Creeks and many other Indians who had fought with England against the United States escaped to the Seminoles in Florida. While the United States was winning the war, the Seminole population of Florida was more than doubling. After the war the hostile Indians fought again and again with whites on the Georgia-Florida border. Many of the conflicts began with white efforts to recapture runaway slaves. The slaveowners could not easily get back their property because Florida was not U.S. territory. In 1814 American troops led by Andrew Jackson marched into Florida. They fought and defeated the Seminoles in what became known as The First Seminole War (1816-1818). (Osceola and his mother were captives for a short time when a part of Jackson's army attacked their village.) The American army also forced the Spanish to yield Florida to the United States in 1819.

After The First Seminole War the U.S. government considered removing the Seminoles to the West. But the idea was rejected for the time because the Indians were scattered throughout Florida's swamps and forests. Instead, the Seminoles were encouraged to move to a reservation in the center of the state. Whites were permitted to settle anywhere else in Florida, and the Indian reservation was policed to keep out slaves. In 1825 Osceola, then the leader of a small group of warriors, moved to the reservation.

The Indians soon discovered that the land in the reservation was poor. They found it difficult to grow crops, so hungry Indians searched elsewhere for food. White men shot them, and the Indians shot back. Slavecatchers continued to prowl among the Seminoles looking for runaways. This brought about more fighting.

According to some stories, Osceola's hatred for the white man grew out of a personal experience with slavecatchers. Morning Dew, Osceola's wife, was the daughter of an Indian chief and a fugitive slave. In such cases, the law said that a child was the same as its mother. Therefore, Morning Dew was considered a runaway slave. One day while Osceola and his wife were shopping for supplies, she was dragged off by slavecatchers. Osceola was helpless at the time, but he swore revenge.

By 1830 new demands were being made by white settlers—especially those who had settled in northern Florida.

In 1835 Osceola refused to sign a treaty which demanded that the Seminoles leave their homes in Florida and move west to Oklahoma.

They wanted the Indians moved out of their way. That year Congress, now under President Andrew Jackson, passed the Indian Removal Act. The act set aside land west of the Mississippi for the Southern Indian tribes. But it did not allow the Indians to decide if they wanted to live on that land. They had to "freely" give up their land in the southeast and move west, or else U.S. troops would make them move. In 1832 several Seminole chiefs signed the Treaty of Payne's Landing. They agreed that all the Seminoles would leave for Indian Territory (later Oklahoma) within three years. Osceola was at Payne's Landing with other young warriors. But he was not one of the handful of Seminole leaders who signed the treaty.

In 1835 the Seminoles were still in Florida. The local Indian agent, General Wiley Thompson, was impatient with their delays. He called the chiefs together to sign another paper. This time Osceola too was asked to make his mark.

Seminoles attack an American army block house during the Second Seminole War.

He refused. According to one report, he slashed his knife through the paper and said, "This is the only treaty I will sign." Osceola was arrested and imprisoned by General Thompson.

Thompson was soon to regret his clash with the Indian leader. A few months after Osceola was released, he and his warriors attacked Thompson. When the Indian agent was found, there were 14 bullet holes in his body. No one doubted who had murdered him.

The murder of Thompson was one of the early events in an eight-year struggle known as The Second Seminole War. Osceola and his warriors stayed in the swamp, making battle difficult for the soldiers. The Indians seldom met the United States forces face to face. Instead they chose to ambush or strike from the rear. Several generals were put in command of the American troops, but not one was able to outwit Osceola.

Osceola in May 1837, during a break in the Second Seminole War. Five months later he was captured under a white flag of truce.

In 1837 Osceola became ill with malaria. Other Seminole leaders, tired of the fight, agreed to come to peace talks. When Osceola regained his strength, he too agreed to give up the struggle. But rumors began to spread. Dark-skinned Seminoles, it was reported, were being captured and sold as slaves. Even more alarming were rumors that Indian war leaders would be executed by the government. Osceola and his warriors decided there were no grounds for peace. Quickly they escaped into the swamp and again began the fight.

Later that same year Osceola again agreed to come to peace talks. An American brigadier general went to his camp near St. Augustine and found him waiting under a white flag of truce. His people were willing to stop the fight, Osceola explained, but they would not move. The general, not satisfied with this offer, quickly arrested the Seminole. Two hundred soldiers suddenly appeared from hiding to capture Osceola and his band.

The war continued without Osceola until many Seminoles either moved westward or deeper into the Everglades, the great swamp of Florida. Meanwhile Osceola was sent to prison at Fort Moultrie near Charleston, South Carolina. He had been sick again at the time of his arrest, and his illness became more and more serious. Osceola refused help from a white doctor named Weedon. In 1838 he died.

Dr. Weedon later wrote an account of Osceola's death. He told how the sick man had asked for his war costume. When he had put on the costume and red war paint, Osceola shook hands with his relatives and the officers in charge. He then lay down and died, his knife in his hand.

Weedon's record seemed objective enough. What he failed to mention, however, was that he himself had ruthlessly cut off the Seminole's head and preserved it. Weedon too wanted his revenge. Indian agent Thompson—killed by Osceola's bullets—had been Weedon's brother-in-law.

Black Hawk

Black Hawk and Keokuk

Black Hawk and Keokuk were jealous rivals. They were both important leaders of the Sauk and Fox Indians—two closely allied tribes who lived in what are today the states of Wisconsin and Illinois. But the two leaders had very different ideas about how to deal with the United States. Keokuk was an appeaser, willing to give up much of the Sauk and Fox lands and rights in return for peace. Black Hawk was an Indian patriot, who resisted the white man's efforts to remove him from his land.

Born in 1767, Black Hawk lived in the village of Saukenuk (later Rock Island, Illinois). He was involved in battles and raids most of his life. As a youth Black Hawk led raids against Cherokee and Osage camps. During the War of 1812 he and his followers joined the British Army under Tecumseh and fought against the American forces.

Keokuk was no warrior. He was known for his ability as a speaker. A younger man than Black Hawk, Keokuk believed that the Indians should adopt some of the ways of white men, and he wanted to live in peace with the United States. He also wanted to become head chief of all the Sauk and Fox tribes. Keokuk refused to join Black Hawk and the British during the War of 1812. But by offering to defend Saukenuk if American forces should attack the village, Keokuk managed to get himself elected war chief in Black Hawk's absence. When Black Hawk returned to Saukenuk, he was surprised and jealous about Keokuk's position.

After the War of 1812, white settlers began to pour into the Illinois country. According to a treaty signed in 1804, the Sauk and Fox Indians had agreed to move westward and leave this land when settlers arrived. But they did not move. Instead the Sauk and Fox caused the government more and more trouble. The whites had scared away much of their game, so the Sauk and Fox raided Sioux hunting grounds. War bands of Sauk and Fox fought with the Sioux, and sometimes white settlers found themselves caught up in the warfare. The trouble became very serious by the 1820s when the Sauk and Fox lands were swarming with settlers.

Keokuk on horseback.

In 1821 Keokuk went to St. Louis to turn in two Indians who had killed a Frenchman. The governor of the Missouri Territory, William Clark, flattered Keokuk and gave him gifts. Clark had made himself a useful friend. A few years later when Clark and other officials began to demand that the Indians move west, Keokuk said he was willing to move across the Mississippi River to Iowa. But Black Hawk refused to move. He declared that the treaty of 1804 was unjust. He claimed that the signers had been given "firewater" before they made their marks on the treaty. The rivalry between Black Hawk and Keokuk grew. Tribesmen sided with one or the other—for or against removal.

In the late summer of 1828 the Indians left Saukenuk to go on their winter hunt. While they were gone, Black Hawk received word that white people had taken over the village and moved into the Indian lodges. He went back to Saukenuk to see for himself. There he found the settlers arguing over the Indians' corn plots. Back at the winter camp, Black Hawk reported on the state of Saukenuk. The head chiefs then decided to follow Keokuk's advice and move west to Iowa. In the spring of 1829 they crossed the Mississippi—but Black Hawk did not. With his followers he went back to Saukenuk.

Black Hawk's people spent two summers in their old village. But more whites had settled there, and it seemed there were quarrels between the white and the red men every day. By the spring of 1831 the governor of Illinois was ready to take action against the Indians. He called up the state militia and asked Clark to send federal troops. Black Hawk was told to take his people west—or else the army would do it.

Early on the morning of June 26, 1831, federal and state troops invaded Saukenuk, only to find that the Indians were already gone. Overnight they had quietly trooped out and crossed the river. The disappointed militia burned down the village.

In Iowa Black Hawk was quiet for awhile. But soon he was working hard to gain the support of neighboring tribes. He was encouraged when he received word that the British and several tribes were ready to help him. In April 1832 Black Hawk with several hundred braves and their families returned to Illinois to reclaim their land. The promised help never came, however. And there were large forces against the Indians—the Illinois militia and the regular army under General Henry Atkinson. Without aid or supplies Black Hawk recognized that he was powerless.

Women and children flee while Black Hawk's warriors fight at the Battle of Bad Axe in 1832. The Indians were ruthlessly massacred.

Admitting defeat, he sent three messengers under a white flag of truce to the nearby militia. But one of the messengers and two other warriors were shot down by the excited volunteer troops. Black Hawk and his braves struck back. They ambushed a pack of soldiers and sent the survivors crashing back into camp, sure that they had been hit by a thousand Indians. Black Hawk had only 40 men with him at the time.

Many of the volunteers went home. And before new troops arrived, Black Hawk moved his people north to Wisconsin. Bands of his warriors, and also ones from neighboring tribes, made savage attacks on white settlements. Soon the army was again in pursuit. Under fire, Black Hawk led his people westward across the Wisconsin River and then overland to the Mississippi. The chief had decided to return to Iowa and to forget about the war.

Hungry, wounded, and exhausted, his dwindling band reached the river and was about to cross when the steamboat *Warrior* appeared. Black Hawk held up a white flag and called out that he wanted to surrender. The troops on board did not understand his message. They began to fire on the Indians, killing 23 of them. Soon after, when the Indians were making another attempt to cross the Mississippi, the army drew up. Caught between the army and the steamboat, most of Black Hawk's warriors, their wives, and their children were slaughtered. Those who managed to cross the river alive were met on the west bank by a band of Sioux who killed or captured them. The Indians' terrible defeat became known as the Battle of Bad Axe. Black Hawk himself escaped. But soon a group of Indians convinced him to go to Prairie du Chien, Wisconsin, where he surrendered on August 27, 1832.

Black Hawk at Jefferson Barracks near St. Louis, where he was imprisoned at the end of the Black Hawk War.

Black Hawk was imprisoned for several months at Jefferson Barracks near St. Louis. Then he and some of his followers were moved to Washington, D.C. They spent a few more weeks in prison there. Then they were taken to meet President Jackson, who gave the old chief a military uniform. The trip ended with a sightseeing tour of the eastern cities. Impressed and pleased, Black Hawk returned home, only to find that the government had made Keokuk head chief of the Sauk and Fox tribes.

Keokuk had taken no part in the Black Hawk War. Indeed he had offered to help the government in its pursuit of Black Hawk. After the war he tried to convince U.S. officials that a large area in what is now Iowa rightfully belonged to the Sauk and Fox. Keokuk won his case and

Keokuk in old age. Although he became head chief of the Sauk and Fox, many of his people considered him a traitor.

claimed the land for the Indians. The disappointed Black Hawk lived in a lodge on Keokuk's reservation during his last years. There he dictated his memoirs. In the autumn of 1836 Keokuk sold to the government huge amounts of the Sauk and Fox lands. While Keokuk proudly signed the treaty and addressed a large group of Indians and government officials, Black Hawk and his sons looked on from the sidelines. Wearing a worn frock coat and a brown hat, the old chief watched the ceremony "in dumb and dismal silence," according to artist George Catlin.

Black Hawk died in 1838 at the age of 71. Today a magnificent statue of him stands in Oregon, Illinois. A city in Iowa was named after Keokuk, who outlived his rival by 10 years.

Crazy Horse swore he would never be photographed, but many people believe this is a portrait of the chief.

Crazy Horse

Ten years after the Black Hawk War, in about 1842, a boy was born in the winter camp of a band of Oglala Teton Sioux, east of the Black Hills. The boy's father, Crazy Horse, was a medicine man. His mother was the sister of a chief, Spotted Tail. The young Indian had a light skin and mild manner. He was often called the Strange One, or Curly. Yet he grew up to be the greatest war chief of the Sioux Nation.

As a boy, Curly made friends with a warrior named Hump, who taught him how to hunt and fight. At 12 Curly had already killed a buffalo and could keep his seat on a wild horse. Late that summer—in 1854—an important event happened in the young boy's life. When the Sioux tribes went to Fort Laramie for supplies, a settler's cow wandered into one of the Sioux camps. In panic the owner reported that the Indians had stolen his cow. Thirty soldiers rushed from the fort to the camp, where they found that the cow had been shot. The troops fired upon the Indians. The Sioux fought back and killed all of the soldiers. Then they packed up and fled to the north.

During a halt in the journey, Curly took his horse and went off by himself. He had been very upset by the fight at Fort Laramie. For three days he lay on a hilltop and waited for a vision. (All Sioux boys were expected to seek a vision of their guardian spirit by fasting alone in the wilderness.) Weak with hunger, at last Curly saw a rider on horseback coming toward him. Arrows flew through the air but did not strike the rider. A small streak of lightning was on his cheek, and his body was covered with marks like hailstones. A small stone rested behind his ear.

A few years later the boy told his father about the dream. His father thought the vision was powerful and meant that his son would not be killed in battle. So the young Sioux went into his first battle marked like the rider he had seen in his vision. Afterwards, his father gave his name—Crazy Horse—to the boy and took for himself the name Worm.

The Sioux had been in conflict with white settlers and troops on and off for most of Crazy Horse's life. But the struggle became greater after the Civil War. Crazy Horse was alarmed by the white man's invasion of the plains. In 1866 he joined forces with an older war chief, Red Cloud.

Red Cloud of the Sioux was the only Indian chief to win a war with the United States.

Working together, the Sioux were determined to stop the government from building forts along the Bozeman Trail. (The trail led to gold that had been discovered in Montana.) For two years the Indians attacked anyone who tried to cross tribal lands. They also held the largest of the government forts under constant siege. Travel in the area was impossible. Government officials finally agreed to abandon the forts and to negotiate with the Indians. When Red Cloud saw the last of the forts burned to the ground, he agreed to sign a treaty. With his victory Red Cloud became the only chief to win a war with the United States.

The signing of the Fort Laramie Treaty between the Sioux and the United States, 1868.

The Fort Laramie Treaty of 1868 brought the Red Cloud War to an end. It also set aside a large reservation for the Sioux—Standing Rock Reservation in what is now South Dakota. The Indians who signed the treaty did not understand—or perhaps were not told—what it really said. For several years many of them resisted the army's attempts to move them. Finally, in 1870 Red Cloud agreed to settle on an agency in Nebraska. But Crazy Horse's band of Oglala Sioux remained on the plains of northern Wyoming and southern Montana.

Colonel George Armstrong Custer (seated), surrounded by some of his Indian scouts. Bloody Knife (kneeling at left) was killed with Custer and his troops at the Battle of the Little Bighorn.

In 1873 Indian fighter George Armstrong Custer and his 7th Cavalry came north. They were to guard the Northern Pacific railway crews who planned to cut through Indian lands. Crazy Horse's band lashed out at Custer, but the railway surveyors were able to finish their work. A year later Custer returned at the head of a huge party of troops, scouts, newsmen, and gold seekers. This time he planned to take a look at the Black Hills. Soon the government was offering to buy the hills from the Sioux. But the Indians did not want to sell, because the beautiful pine-forested region was sacred land to them.

In December 1875 the government ordered all the Sioux to enter reservations by January 1876 or face the consequences. By the time Crazy Horse received the message, winter had set in and the Indians faced severe cold and possible starvation. Travel was nearly impossible. But in February the problem of rounding up the Indian bands was turned over to the military. In March U.S. troops under the command of General George Crook attacked a band of Cheyennes camped not far from Crazy Horse. The Indians were forced to flee into the hills, but when the women and children were safe in Crazy Horse's camp, the warriors struck back. Crook's troops remained long enough to set fire to the Cheyenne camp. Then they hurried away to join the rest of his forces on the Powder River. The Cheyenne and Sioux Indians continued to snipe at the soldiers and to steal their horses and cattle. Soon Crook had to leave the Powder River in defeat.

That spring Crazy Horse (who had just been named head chief of the Oglala Teton Sioux) began to prepare for a major battle. His band was joined by the Cheyennes, by the Hunkpapa Teton Sioux led by Sitting Bull, and by the Hunkpapa Teton Sioux under Chief Gall. Many other Sioux from the reservations also joined Crazy Horse. The Indians set up camp on the west bank of the Little Bighorn River in southern Montana. There were about 12,000 to 15,000 Indians in the camp—5,000 of them warriors.

In June Sitting Bull, the trusted Sioux medicine man, had a vision of soldiers falling into the Indian camp. Soon Crazy Horse heard that General Crook was on his way up the Rosebud River. With 1,000 warriors he left the Indian camp on the Little Bighorn and met Crook on the Rosebud. They fought all day until the Indians ran low on bullets and galloped back to camp. Crook, who had sustained many losses, retreated to the south. By this time the army knew that rounding up the Sioux would be no easy task. What the troops didn't know was that their greatest defeat was yet to come. The Battle of the Little Bighorn was fought a week later, on June 25, 1876.

A white artist's idea of the Battle of the Little Bighorn. Custer (center) is drawn as a heroic figure holding a white flag.

From the east Lieutenant George Custer and his troops moved into the valley of the Little Bighorn. Custer sent one detachment to cross the river and attack the Indian camp from the south. These forces were led by Major Marcus Reno. Another detachment under Captain Frederick Benteen was to follow Reno and Custer and serve as a reinforcement. With 224 men Custer himself moved north on the eastern bank. But the Indians knew of Custer's approach. Sitting Bull and Chief Gall with their forces drove Major Reno's troops back across the river. The Indians under Chief Gall then rode north after Custer along the eastern bank of the Little Bighorn.

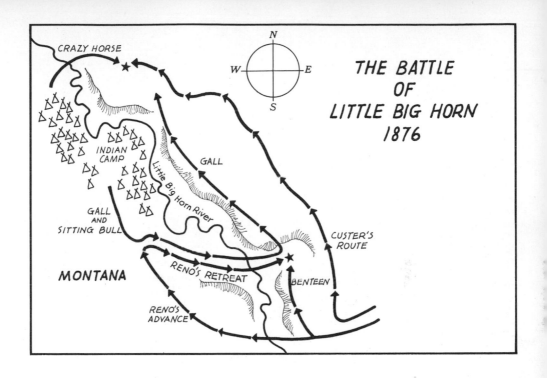

Crazy Horse was commander-in-chief of all Indian forces, including those of Sitting Bull and Chief Gall. When Reno began his attack on the south end of the Indian camp, Crazy Horse was in the north. He saw Custer on the east bank of the river, preparing to cross over. Crazy Horse marked a small zigzag that looked like lightning on his face and marks like hailstones on his body. Then he tied a stone to his head. The young chief led his warriors into battle shouting, "Today is a good day to fight! Today is a good day to die!" The Indians attacked Custer on the east bank of the Little Bighorn and flew at him from all directions. Within an hour Custer's entire force was wiped out. The Indians fought off Reno's and Benteen's men for another day, until they were warned that more troops were coming.

Then they set fire to the prairie grass. Hidden by gusts of smoke, they gathered up their belongings and headed south for the Bighorn Mountains.

The defeat of Custer and his men confirmed Crazy Horse's reputation as one of the greatest Indian leaders of all time. But the Indians' glory faded soon after the famous battle. Their greatest victory was also their last one. The Sioux and Cheyenne forces broke up and spread out or returned to the agencies for the winter. There the chiefs were forced to sign over the Black Hills and their hunting lands farther west. The army set out to bring in those Indians still at large.

Several times Crazy Horse was attacked by Colonel Nelson Miles, but each time the troops were pushed back. Finally, in the spring of 1877, Crazy Horse was forced to surrender. The chief's army was smaller because many of his warriors had deserted. During a bitter winter his people had been threatened by starvation. Defeated but still proud, they marched to the Red Cloud Agency in war costume.

In the Black Hills of South Dakota, Korczak Ziolkowski stands below his model for a statue of *Crazy Horse.* Since 1951 he has been carving the gigantic statue into the mountain behind him.

Death came to Crazy Horse soon after he entered the reservation. Warned by Crazy Horse's enemies that the chief would stir up trouble, General Crook ordered him to be locked up. As Crazy Horse struggled to break away, a guard stabbed him in the back with a bayonet. A few hours later he was dead.

Chief Gall

Gall

The Battle of the Little Bighorn is linked most often with the names of Crazy Horse and Sitting Bull. But Chief Gall, leader of a Hunkpapa Teton Sioux tribe, was also responsible for Custer's defeat.

Gall was born around 1840 and was given the Indian name of Pizi. One day while hunting with his young friends, he tried to swallow the gall (a digestive fluid usually called "bile") of a slain animal. Whether or not he succeeded is not really known. But he did succeed in earning the name Gall for the rest of his life.

Like Sitting Bull and other chiefs, Gall refused to enter the reservation during the last troubled years of the Sioux Nation. Instead he and his band roamed the plains. Eventually they joined Crazy Horse and Sitting Bull at the Little Big Horn, where Gall first fought Reno, then led his forces across the river and up the eastern bank after Custer. When the Sioux were later forced to retreat, Gall escaped with Sitting Bull into Canada. However, Chief Gall's ideas were different from those of the great medicine man, and they had several disputes. During the bitter winter of 1880, Gall went back across the border, surrendered, and entered a reservation.

An Indian picture of the Battle of the Little Bighorn, done 22 years after the battle. The four figures standing in the center are (left to right) Sitting Bull, Rain-in-the-Face, Crazy Horse, and the artist himself, Kicking Bear. Chief Gall, who had an important part in the battle, was left out of the drawing because he later became friendly with whites.

Chief Gall accepted the defeat of the Sioux with much less bitterness than many other Indian leaders. Once on the reservation he settled down to farming. Yet he did not lose his strength and dignity as a leader. He worked to keep affairs running smoothly between the Sioux and the Indian agent, McLaughlin. When the peace seemed threatened by a new Indian religion that came to be called the Ghost Dance, Gall spoke against the Ghost Dance at council meetings. The Sioux, he believed, would not find answers to their problems in the frenzied dance of the new religion. He begged them to return to the schools and churches established for them by white men. There, he pleaded, they would

find their only answers. They must learn to face a new way of life. In 1889 Gall was appointed a judge in the Indian Court of the Standing Rock Reservation.

When Chief Gall died in 1894, he received a warm tribute from Custer's widow. After seeing a portrait of Gall, she wrote a message to the photographer. ". . . I never dreamed in all my life, there could be so fine a specimen of a warrior . . . as Chief Gall." However, many Indians came to see Gall as a traitor because of his friendship in late years with the white man.

Sitting Bull

Sitting Bull

Sitting Bull was not the greatest chief in history. He was not the boldest warrior. Yet he is the best remembered. No one recalls Custer's last stand without thinking of Sitting Bull. No one describes Buffalo Bill's Wild West Show without mentioning Sitting Bull. The portraits of the firm old chief have come to remind people of all the Indians who put down their weapons but never gave up the fight.

Sitting Bull, chief of a Hunkpapa Teton Sioux tribe, was born in South Dakota in about 1831. At the age of 14 he was on the warpath, fighting the Crow Indians and making his name as a warrior. He also became highly respected among Sioux tribes as a medicine man.

The last half of the 19th century was a time of great struggle for Sitting Bull, his people, and the entire Sioux Nation. Settlers were moving westward across the plains. Prospectors swarmed into and across Indian lands when gold was discovered in the West. White hunters were killing off the buffalo—the Sioux's main source of food, clothing, and shelter. The United States made treaties with the Sioux and then usually broke them. No treaties seemed satisfactory to the government for long because what the United States really wanted was to put the wandering Sioux on reservations and keep them there.

Indians of the Plains depended upon the buffalo for survival. In 1870 as many as 7 million buffalo existed; in 1883 only 200 could be found. The animals disappeared as white men slaughtered them for hides and for sport.

Sitting Bull and his warriors refused to move onto reservations. For several years they were almost constantly on the warpath, attacking settlers and soldiers. The U.S. Army was also on the warpath. In 1876 Sitting Bull and his followers joined forces with Crazy Horse and other Sioux chiefs. The medicine man participated in the Indians' greatest victory—the Battle of the Little Bighorn. Sitting Bull did not, however, take part in the attack on Custer's detachment.

After the famous battle, when troops were sent out to roundup all the Sioux, Sitting Bull escaped into Canada, where he stayed until 1881. At that time he surrendered and was put away for two years as a prisoner of war at Fort Randall in South Dakota. In 1883 he was placed on the Standing Rock Reservation.

For the most part, Sitting Bull stayed on the reservation for the rest of his life. Yet his hatred for the white man was clear in spite of his surrender. He brooded over his fate and dreamed of the days when he and his warriors were free to roam the plains. His attitude angered James McLaughlin, the agent in charge of the reservation. Agent McLaughlin called Sitting Bull greedy and dishonest and said he had never known the Indian to do anything that could be admired.

Sitting Bull did not stir such contempt in all whites, however. In 1883 he was asked to make a speech at the ceremony opening the Northern Pacific Railroad's transcontinental track. (The Chief told the white audience they were thieves and liars. But the "translator" made up some flowery phrases. He did not report Sitting Bull's words.) In 1885 the Sioux chief agreed to join Buffalo Bill Cody's Wild West Show for a season and became a major attraction. As he toured the country he was given a chance to relive the days of the Indians' more glamorous past. Sitting Bull and other Indians staged attacks on wagons and stagecoaches, much to the delight of audiences.

Another white who did not share McLaughlin's feeling was a lady named Catherine Weldon. Mrs. Weldon journeyed to the reservation from the East, determined to paint the aging chief's portrait. For a time she even lived with Sitting Bull and his two wives. Perhaps no one was quite as amazed as the old Sioux himself.

Sitting Bull and Buffalo Bill Cody.
The chief was a member of Cody's
Wild West Show in 1885.

    Mrs. Weldon had chosen a bad time to try to establish a lasting relationship with Sitting Bull and his family. A new religion, called the Ghost Dance, had swept through the Sioux reservations. The prophet of this religion, a Paiute Indian named Wovoka, said that songs and dances would help the Indians in their trouble. Wovoka promised that the dances would bring back the buffalo, raise up dead Indians, and make the white men disappear. Most of the Ghost Dancers wore patterned "ghost shirts" which were supposed to protect them from the white man's bullets. White residents in the Dakotas became alarmed at the sight of the dancers, and soon 3,000 troops were called to the scene.

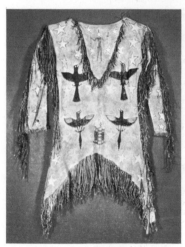

Above, a group of Indian Ghost Dancers. Late in the 19th century many Sioux became followers of the Ghost Dance, a new religion that promised to cure all the troubles caused by the white man. *Left*, a ghost shirt like those worn by Ghost Dancers. Such shirts were supposed to protect their wearers from the white man's bullets.

Mrs. Weldon begged Sitting Bull not to take part in the Ghost Dance. She believed that he could stop the trouble that was certain to come. Surely if the great medicine man refused to support such a religion, hundreds of others would be discouraged from participating in it.

Burial of Indian men, women, and children massacred at the Battle of Wounded Knee—the last major battle between white men and red men.

Flattered as Sitting Bull may have been by Catherine Weldon's great admiration for him, he was not about to bend to her wishes. He took part in the dances, and Mrs. Weldon left. Misfortune met the artist on her return trip, however. When her son died aboard the steamboat, she wrote to the Sioux chief saying that she wished she had never left, ". . . for then I would have buried him there and remained near my Indians. Now I am far from all my Dakota friends and from you, and my only child gone too. Nothing left to me. . . ." She continued, "When death comes to both of us we may not be eternally separated, but meet again in a better world."

Soon after, in December 1890, death came to Sitting Bull. To stop the spread of the Ghost Dance, McLaughlin decided that the still-hostile chief should be arrested. When the police, who were Indians themselves, came to take Sitting Bull away, he refused to go with them. One of his angry followers shot the arresting officer. In response the police fatally shot Sitting Bull.

Burying the dead after the Battle of Wounded Knee, S.D. -1890.

After Sitting Bull's death, a band of Sioux led by Big Foot fled the reservation and disappeared into the Badlands. There they were rounded up by the 7th Cavalry (Custer's old unit) and taken to Wounded Knee Creek. When the colonel asked them to disarm, one Indian fired his gun and wounded an officer. The troops opened fire upon the band of Indians. Two hundred men, women, and children thought they were safe in their bulletproof ghost shirts. They all fell dead. The soldiers left the bodies to freeze on the cold earth for three days. Later they insisted that when they fired, it had been hard to tell the women from the men. The American government gave the Medal of Honor to 18 of the soldiers for their action at Wounded Knee.

Cochise

Cochise

While the Sioux struggled with the whites on the Great Plains, the Indians of the Southwest were having similar problems. After the end of the Mexican War in 1848, settlers began moving rapidly into what later became Arizona and New Mexico. As usual, many of the whites took over with little concern for the Indians. They paid a high price for their actions. The Indians struck back with savage attacks on both settlers and soldiers in the territory.

In the 1850s an Apache chief named Cochise made peace with the settlers. Warfare ended for several years. Cochise and his band even went to work with the Butterfield Stage Coach Line. Cochise himself provided firewood for the stagecoach station. Then one day in 1861 a settler's child was kidnapped. Cochise was alarmed. If his people were blamed for the kidnapping, the peace would be broken.

Cochise and five other chiefs were called to meet with the 7th Cavalry. The Indians hoped to convince the troops of their innocence in the matter. As Cochise and his companions rode up to the cavalry camp, they saw a white flag of truce flying from the commander's tent. But once they were inside the tent, the Indians had questions thrown at them—and demands that they confess to the crime. When they refused to confess, the commander had them arrested and announced that they would be hanged the following morning. One of the Apaches was shot and killed on the spot. Cochise sliced his way out the side of the tent. He was shot three times as he escaped, but his companions were not so lucky. They were hanged without a trial. Cochise was furious and promised revenge. Thus began a long, bitter war.

Cochise proved to be a brilliant war chief. Soon his name was heard wherever people discussed Indian problems. One reporter described the chief as a man with "broad shoulders; stout frame; eyes medium size and very black; hair straight; scarred all over the body with buckshot. . . ."

The Civil War partly interrupted the Indian war in the Southwest. Many soldiers left to fight on new battlefields. Cochise did not know about the War Between the States. He was sure that he had forced the Army to retreat, and he concluded that his people could be victorious if they fought fiercely enough. With the soldiers gone, he turned his attention to the unprotected settlers. His attacks, according to some stories, were swift and savage.

In the autumn of 1861 a group of Union army volunteers from California had to pass through Apache country. The soldiers were on their way to fight the Confederates in New Mexico. High in the mountains, Cochise and a band of about 500 warriors were waiting to ambush them. The battle raged for a whole day until the troops dragged up their howitzers and fired on the Indians. These small cannons where the first artillery pieces to be used against the Apaches. The army killed many Indians with their cannon, and drove the rest of them away.

Cochise's hideaway in the Cragoon Mountains of Arizona.

When regular troops returned to the Southwest, they pressed hard after the Apaches. Some bands were nearly wiped out. But at the same time a man named Thomas J. Jeffords was winning the trust of Cochise. Jefford's job was to see that the mail was carried safely through the area.

This man has been identified as Cochise's son, Naiche, who led his father's band of Apaches after his death, and also as Tahya, the eldest son of Cochise.

He needed the help of the chief, so he rode to the Apache camp and talked with Cochise. The two men became good friends. In 1872 General Oliver O. Howard took Jeffords along on a treaty-making expedition to Cochise's mountain hideaway. Jeffords was able to convince the Apache to surrender. In return Cochise and his people were permitted to live in their native territory—on a reservation of their choice. Cochise also asked that Jeffords be named Indian agent.

In 1874 Cochise died while visiting Jeffords. His warriors took the chief's scarred body into the mountains to be buried away from white men. It has never been found. Not long after Cochise's death the federal government broke its promise and moved his band to another reservation.

Geronimo

Geronimo

One day a band of Mexicans swept into an Apache camp. The raid had a striking effect on a young Indian, and eventually on the history of the Southwest. The easy-going youth was called Goyathlay, meaning "One Who Yawns." After the raid Goyathlay's mild ways changed. His entire family had been killed. The youth swore to take revenge against all Mexicans. He became known to them as Geronimo—a name that came to be feared on both sides of the border.

For about 15 years Geronimo sought his revenge. He and his band of Apaches made raids into northern Mexico, killing and looting as they went. Then in 1876 Geronimo turned his anger on Americans. The United States government decided to move his band of Apaches from their mountain home in southeast Arizona to the flat, dry land of the San Carlos Reservation. But Geronimo wasn't willing to try to farm on such terrible soil. He and his band escaped into the mountains of Mexico. From there they raided and terrorized the country around Tucson, Arizona.

A meeting in 1886 between Geronimo (far left) and General George Crook (far right). Geronimo was captured twice by Crook, and twice he managed to escape.

In 1883 Geronimo's raids came to an end, at least for a short time. He was defeated by General George Crook—the Crook who had been defeated by Crazy Horse at the Rosebud River. Geronimo and his followers were sent to the reservation. For two years the war-minded chief settled down to farming. But his bloody career was not over. Geronimo escaped.

General Crook's forces moved into Mexico in hot pursuit. For the second time Geronimo surrendered to Crook. But he escaped even before his captors reached the United States border. Crook was embarrassed. He withdrew from the campaign and was replaced by General Nelson Miles. Miles set off with 5,000 troops to search for Geronimo.

Apache men, women, and children in Geronimo's camp in the Sierra Madre of Mexico in 1886.

In 1886 one of Miles's lieutenants found Geronimo's camp in the wilds of Mexico. The chief's band had dwindled to about 20 warriors and their families. Geronimo was persuaded to surrender. The Army then rounded up the peaceful Apaches who had remained at San Carlos, and even the Apache scouts who had helped General Crook. They were all put into wagons along with Geronimo and his band. Then the Indians were shipped by railway east to Florida as prisoners of war. Later they were moved to Alabama, and finally to Fort Sill, Oklahoma.

Geronimo (third from right) and other Apaches waiting to be shipped from Arizona to Florida as prisoners of war, 1886.

The aging chief changed drastically in his final years. At Fort Sill he became a successful farmer. He also became a Christian and joined the Dutch Reformed Church. Geronimo had become famous for his savage career. In 1904 he made special appearances at the St. Louis World's Fair, and the next year he rode in Teddy Roosevelt's inaugural parade. In 1906 his autobiography was published.

In old age, Geronimo lived on the reservation at Fort Sill, Oklahoma.

Geronimo died in 1909 at the age of 80. Forty years of his long life had been spent in burning, looting, and killing. He had certainly won his revenge for the massacre of his family. For a long time after his death his name was a symbol for terror and destruction.

Chief Joseph

Joseph

The Nez Percé Indians were a peaceful tribe. In 1805 they had welcomed the members of the Lewis and Clark expedition to their home in the Northwest. After that the Nez Percé wanted trade—not trouble—with the white man. For the most part they were content to hunt and fish and raise large herds of beautiful Appaloosa horses.

But white men could change the ways of even the most peaceful Indians. As the Northwest began to be settled, the Nez Percé agreed to give up most of their land. A treaty in 1855 allowed them to keep only a section in Oregon and some high grasslands in Idaho.

Then in 1863 gold was discovered on one of the Nez Percé reservations in Oregon. The Indians were asked to move to a new reservation and give up more of their territory. Part of the Nez Percé tribe did move, but one old chief's band stayed. In 1871 the chief died and his son Joseph became leader of the band. Homesteaders poured into their valley, the beautiful grassy region of the Wallowa River in northeastern Oregon. Quietly but firmly Chief Joseph refused to leave. He remembered his father's words: "This country holds your father's body. Never sell the bones of your father and mother."

Chief Joseph was at this time a handsome man in his early thirties. He had studied at a mission school and knew something about the white man's ways and about his language. But Joseph did not yet know just how powerful and determined the white man really was. For a time it seemed the government could not decide what to do about the Nez Percé. In 1873 the Grant administration declared that the Wallowa Valley belonged to the Indians—but the settlers did not leave. Then in 1875 the government changed its mind and opened the valley to white settlement. Two years later the Nez Percé were told they had to leave their valley. If they did not leave on their own, they would be moved by force.

Joseph had second thoughts about his refusal to move. The government was putting great pressure on his tribe and others who had stayed in the valley. And Joseph did not want war. Also, the Army had captured an important religious leader of the Nez Percé. The Army offered to release the leader if Joseph would move within 30 days. Joseph and his people began to prepare for the journey.

Looking Glass was one of the greatest war chiefs of the Nez Percés. Like so many of his people, he was killed in 1877 during the famous retreat under Chief Joseph.

In mid-June 1877 the tribe was on its way to the reservation. But a group of young warriors forced a sudden change in Joseph's plans. The braves got drunk and went on the warpath, killing several white settlers in the area. Chief Joseph still did not want war, and he offered to surrender the guilty warriors to the Army. But it was too late. A group of soldiers sent by General Oliver O. Howard fired on the Indians in their hideout in White Bird Canyon. The fighting began.

The Nez Percés under Chief Joseph traveled over 1,000 miles in 115 days, trying to escape into Canada. Stars on the map indicate where battles took place between the Nez Percés and pursuing U.S. troops. The Indians were captured by Colonel Nelson Miles only 30 miles from the border.

The Nez Percé led Howard's troops on a chase through the wilds of southern Idaho and then began one of the most famous retreats in American history. The Indians knew they could never regain their own land, but they did not want to surrender. Under Joseph's leadership they determined to escape—first to Montana and then north to Canada. So the chief began his impossible journey—with women, children, the sick, the aged, and the tribe's herd of 2,000 horses in his care. For 115 days the band struggled over rugged mountain passes, while Joseph's war chiefs battled the pursuing troops. Cavalry from posts further east also attacked the Indians. As the Nez Percé band passed through Yellowstone Park they picked up a group of

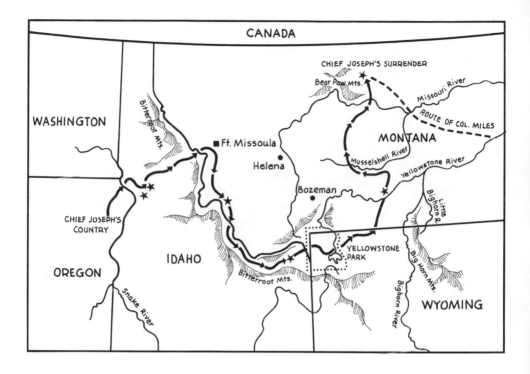

tourists and carried them along for some distance. The
Indians treated the tourists well and let them go before
leaving Yellowstone, then in its fifth year as a national park.

Finally, after traveling more than 1,000 miles, the
Indians could go no farther. They were resting only 30 miles
from the Canadian border when they were attacked by fresh
troops commanded by Colonel Nelson Miles. (The year
before Miles had been engaged chasing Crazy Horse across
the plains.) With Miles's troops in the front and the forces
of General Howard approaching from the rear, the warriors
were outnumbered two to one.

Chief Joseph in old age. Like so many Indian leaders, he only wanted the white man to leave him alone and let his people live their lives in peace.

After a desperate battle the Nez Percé surrendered on October 13, 1877. Chief Joseph made his speech of surrender to Colonel Miles:

Tell General Howard I know his heart. What he told me before I have in my heart. I am tired of fighting. Our chiefs are killed.... The old men are all dead.... It is cold and we have no blankets. The little children are freezing to death. My people, some of them, have run away to the hills and have no blankets, no food; no one knows where they are—perhaps freezing to death. I want to have time to look for my children and see how many I can find. Maybe I shall find them among the dead. Hear me, my chiefs. I am tired; my heart is sick and sad. From where the sun now stands, I will fight no more forever.

Nespelem on the Colville Reservation in Washington, where Chief Joseph spent the last days of his life.

The Nez Percé were sent to Kansas and later to Indian Territory in Oklahoma. Worn, ill, and far from their home, most of them died. Finally, public opinion demanded that they be sent to more familiar country. Thus they were moved again, this time to the Colville Reservation in northern Washington. Joseph tried to get back to the Wallowa Valley, but he was not allowed to return.

Chief Joseph died in Washington in 1904. He was among the last of the famous Indian chiefs who had waged war with the whites. Although the Indians would still continue to struggle for their rights, their wars with the whites were over: "From where the sun now stands, I will fight no more forever."

The Pull Ahead Books

AMERICA'S FIRST LADIES
   1789 to 1865
AMERICA'S FIRST LADIES
   1865 to the Present Day
DARING SEA CAPTAINS
DOERS AND DREAMERS
FAMOUS CHESS PLAYERS
FAMOUS CRIMEFIGHTERS
FAMOUS SPIES
GREAT AMERICAN NATURALISTS
INDIAN CHIEFS
PIRATES AND BUCCANEERS
POLITICAL CARTOONISTS
PRESIDENTIAL LOSERS
SINGERS OF THE BLUES
STARS OF THE ZIEGFELD FOLLIES
WESTERN LAWMEN
WESTERN OUTLAWS

We specialize in publishing quality books for
young people. For a complete list please write

LERNER PUBLICATIONS COMPANY

241 First Avenue North, Minneapolis, Minnesota 55401